TXT ME L8R

Using Technology Responsibly

ABDO
Publishing Company

TXT ME L8R

Using Technology Responsibly

by Ashley Rae Harris

Content Consultant
Dr. Robyn J. A. Silverman
Child/Teen Development Expert and Success Coach
Powerful Words Character Development

Credits

Published by ABDO Publishing Company, 8000 West 78th Street, Edina, Minnesota 55439. Copyright © 2010 by Abdo Consulting Group, Inc. International copyrights reserved in all countries. No part of this book may be reproduced in any form without written permission from the publisher. The Essential Library™ is a trademark and logo of ABDO Publishing Company.

Printed in the United States.

Editor: Amy Van Zee
Copy Editor: Melissa Johnson
Interior Design and Production: Emily Love
Cover Design: Becky Daum

Library of Congress Cataloging-in-Publication Data
Harris, Ashley Rae.
  Txt me l8r : using technology responsibly / by Ashley Rae Harris ; content consultant: Dr. Robyn J.A. Silverman.
      p. cm. — (Essential health : strong, beautiful girls)
  Includes index.
  ISBN 978-1-60453-754-3
  1. Information technology—Social aspects. 2. Technological innovations—Social aspects. 3. Technology—Social aspects. 4. Internet—Social aspects. I. Title. II. Title: Text me later.

  HM851.H367 2010
  303.48'33083—dc22

                                2009002138

 Manufactured with paper containing at least 10% post-consumer waste

Contents

Meet Dr. Robyn

Dr. Robyn Silverman loves to spend time with young people. It's what she does best! As a child and adolescent development specialist, Dr. Robyn has devoted her time to helping girls just like you become all they can be. Throughout the Strong, Beautiful Girls series, you'll hear her expert advice as she offers wisdom on boyfriends, school, and everything in between.

An award-winning body image expert and the creator of the Powerful Words Character System, Dr. Robyn likes to look on the bright side of life. She knows how tough it is to be a young woman in today's world, and she's prepared with encouragement to help you embrace your beauty even when your "frenemies" tell you otherwise. Dr. Robyn struggled with her own body image while growing up, so she knows what you're going through.

Dr. Robyn has been told she has a rare talent—to help girls share their wildest dreams and biggest problems. Her compassion makes her a trusted friend to many girls, and she considers it a gift to be able to interact with the young people who she sees as the leaders of tomorrow. She even started a girls' group, the Sassy Sisterhood Girls Circle, to help young women pinpoint how media messages impact their lives and body confidence so they can get healthy and get happy.

As a speaker and a success coach, her powerful messages have reached thousands of people. Her expert advice has been featured in Prevention magazine, Parents magazine, and the Washington Post. She was even a guest editor for the Dove Self-Esteem Fund: Campaign for Real Beauty. But she has an online presence too, and her writing can be found through her blogs, www.DrRobynsBlog.com and www.BodyImageBlog.com, or through her Web site, www.DrRobynSilverman.com. Dr. Robyn also enjoys spending time with her family in Massachusetts.

Dr. Robyn believes that young people are assets to be developed, not problems to be fixed. She's out to help you become the best you can be. As she puts it, "I'm stepping up to the plate to highlight news stories gone wrong, girls gone right, and programs that help to support strengths instead of weaknesses. I'd be grateful if you'd join me."

Take It from Me

Technology is fun. What girl doesn't like receiving pictures via e-mail or cell phone? But although it is fun, technology is also time-consuming. When you really think about it, how many hours do you spend IM-ing or texting your friends, playing Wii tennis or Guitar Hero, shopping for a cute pair of jeans online, catching your favorite show on television, or checking your Facebook profile? Some days, you probably do all of the above. In addition to the technology used in your free time, maybe your teachers even use online learning tools at school. We're lucky that there are so many different kinds of technology available to us for so many different purposes. But we have to be careful not to get so sucked into our virtual games, shopping, and communicating that we forget what it's like to talk to real people in person or go outside to walk around in the real world.

Technology can be addictive. Some kids get so involved with their online friends and communities that they'd rather stay in than go out with their friends from school. Other kids are so into a game, they feel the need to play it all the time. A lot of young girls, in particular, can become susceptible to online predators through chat rooms and online communities. Because they don't actually see the person face-to-face, they have no way to make sure that online friends are who they say they are.

Why do some people prefer living on one side of a computer screen instead of in the real world? Where do you draw the line between normal usage of technology and addiction? In this book, we will do our best to answer these questions and more. We will also help you set guidelines for having safe fun with technology. There are tons of cool games and communities available to us through computers, televisions, and phones—but they should add to our lives, not consume them.

XOXO,
Ashley

1

The Facebook Era

Pretty much everyone I know has a Facebook or MySpace profile: friends, coworkers, cousins, even my dad! Our online profiles have become such a huge part of our lives that it is sometimes difficult to separate them from our offline personalities. If these communities seem natural to adults, they are even more so for kids who have grown up accessing personal online profiles and communities every day.

There are many great things about having a profile on Facebook, MySpace, or other online communities. A girl can chat with her friends, post photos of her pets for her classmates to see, find a friend she met at summer camp, or check to see if the guy she just started going out with has changed his status yet.

There are also some not-so-fun things about online communities. Some girls get so into checking their profile and sending messages online that they forget to have fun in "real time," such as talking to the friends who are sitting right next to them. Other girls may develop a look or identity online that differs from how they are in person. Others might expose too much information about themselves, leaving them vulnerable to attack from either judgmental peers or shady Internet predators trolling for troubled kids on adolescent-dominated sites. Olivia learned the hard way that getting sucked in online can end up causing real trouble offline.

> **Some girls get so into checking their profile and sending messages online that they forget to have fun in "real time," such as talking to the friends who are sitting right next to them.**

Olivia's Story

Olivia was super good with computers. She knew how to create Web sites and troubleshoot most problems. She often had to teach her parents how to do things that had become simple to her, such as downloading photos or installing new software.

Olivia had profiles on every online community site you could think of: MySpace, Facebook, Friendster, Xanga . . . you name it. She could check her profiles on her cell phone or her personal laptop, and she was constantly updating her photos and information. She updated her profiles so frequently that it was sometimes hard to think of new and interesting things to post.

Talk About It

- **Do you have any online profiles? What do you like or dislike about them?**

- **How often do you check and update your online profile(s)?**

- **Have you ever had trouble thinking of something new to post?**

The first thing Olivia did when she woke up in the morning or got home from school and the last thing she did before she went to bed was log on to each of her different profiles to see if anything had happened since she last checked. Occasionally, she checked them on her cell phone during the day, but she had to be careful not to get her phone taken by a teacher.

Olivia spent so much time online that she had even started to turn down her friends' invitations to

hang out. Most of her free time after school and on the weekends was spent chatting with people online and reading their profiles and blog entries. She probably knew more about her classmates

Olivia spent so much time online that she had even started to turn down her friends' invitations to hang out.

from what they posted than from actual conversations she'd had with them. There were even people she chatted with online that she never said hello to when she passed them in the hallway at school.

There was one guy who Olivia chatted with online named Mike. He was two years younger than Olivia, but he was almost as big of a Facebook user as she was. Olivia knew that if she logged on, nine times out of ten, Mike would be logged on too.

They talked about all kinds of stuff, such as how much they disliked one particular teacher, or what their favorite movies were. Once, when they were chatting for a long time, Olivia even told him about how she was bummed out that Jeff Gunther, the boy she had a crush on, had asked a different girl to go out with him.

Talk About It

- **Do you have any online friends whom you don't talk to or hang out with offline?**

- **What do you like about your online friendships, and how are they different from your offline friendships?**

- **Could an online-only friend ever become a true offline friend? Why or why not?**

One afternoon, when Olivia checked her Facebook profile, she noticed that Mike had posted a comment:

"Don't worry about Gunther. You'll find someone better because you're awesome!"

Olivia was mortified! What if Jeff Gunther had seen the comment about him? What if someone else from her class had seen it? She deleted it as quickly as she could, then fired off a message to Mike just as quickly:

"Mike, don't ever write a comment about something personal about me ever again! YOU DON'T EVEN KNOW ME!"

Olivia tried to calm down, but she couldn't stop worrying about what people might think if they had seen Mike's comment.

Talk About It

- Have you ever had someone post something embarrassing on your online profile? How did you feel and what did you do?

- Why do you think Olivia reacted the way she did? Do you think it was fair for her to tell Mike that he doesn't even know her?

For the rest of the night, Olivia kept checking her profile and Jeff Gunther's obsessively, wondering if he had seen the comment.

Eventually, she had a message in her inbox. She breathed in sharply, thinking it must be something nasty from Jeff or someone else at school.

Instead it was from Mike: "Olivia, I didn't mean to upset you. I thought we were friends, but I guess we aren't."

Suddenly, Olivia felt terrible about the message she sent to Mike. She realized that even though it was kind of dumb that he posted the message for everyone to see, he hadn't posted it to embarrass her. He was actually trying to make her feel better about her crush. Olivia felt even worse when she realized it was all her fault. She had been sharing personal information with people online who she didn't know very well, and a private fact had become public on her Facebook profile. Olivia knew she needed to be more guarded about what she told people while chatting online.

Talk About It

- **What would you do if you were Olivia? Would you say something to Mike?**

- **Have you ever gotten so involved in your online life that you stopped paying attention to your life offline? What made you realize that this was happening?**

Many kids become overly involved in their online life to the point that they stop focusing on their life outside their Internet profiles. Even though chatting and posting comments within online communities can be a fun social experience in moderation, it can become unhealthy if it replaces face-to-face interaction with other kids or family members. Olivia's embarrassment over Mike's comment was the wake-up call she needed. Her over-involvement online was actually clouding her decisions about when and with whom she shared her most personal information.

Remember that when you post a public comment online, everyone can see it. If you have something private to tell someone, instead of commenting online, send him or her an e-mail— or better yet, call your friend. Even though Mike didn't mean to expose Olivia's crush online, he could have been more cautious about what he posted on her profile. If you're not sure if what you're posting is private or would embarrass anyone, don't risk it.

Get Healthy

1. The next time you are browsing an online community, take a second to ask yourself how you are feeling. Are you bored or lonely? If so, think of one other thing you could do to

make yourself feel less bored or lonely that is not online and give it a try.

2. Make a rule with your friends that you will not spend the entire time online when you are visiting one another's homes. Instead, find a game to play, dress up in funny clothes, or make a mix CD of your favorite songs.

3. Double-check what you post online before you hit the send button. Don't be surprised if things seem different from the way you originally intended.

The Last Word from Ashley

It's important to strike a balance between never going online and spending so much of your time online that you forget to actually hang out and talk with your friends and classmates face-to-face. If it starts to become stressful or is taking up all your time, then it's not just a fun way to keep in touch with friends anymore—it's become an obsession, and it may be time to take a break. You might find that after all that time browsing profile pages, it actually feels good to talk to someone else in person.

2

Cyber Bully

One of the drawbacks of being in school is that other kids can be pretty mean. No matter what school you go to, there will always be at least a few bullies. Usually, kids become bullies in groups, ganging up on one or a few people in order to show that they are part of the clique. Unfortunately, bullies also find ways to use new forms of technology to harass their victims. Some bullies find that access to the Internet has provided an opportunity to take typical adolescent bullying to new heights of cruelty.

Most girls have been on the giving, receiving, or both ends of online bullying. Perhaps they've posted a mean joke about someone, visited an unpopular classmate's profile on-line specifically to make fun of it, or found out that a friend had spread rumors about them through e-mail. Even though it might seem funny when someone else is being targeted, an online bully can just as quickly find herself a victim of mean Web games—just take it from Suzy.

Suzy's Story

Suzy was known as a joker at school. She could always be counted on to make a sarcastic remark under her breath that would get other kids snickering in class. Suzy felt most comfortable and popular when she was making other people crack up, and she would do al-most anything for a laugh.

Her blog was no excep-tion. At first, it started with Suzy posting bizarre and hilarious videos she found on YouTube or amusing drawings she doodled dur-ing class. But after a while, she started to post jokes and embarrassing stories about other people. At first, she just made fun of lame people on television, but she soon started to run out of funny things to post. Later, she started to write about teachers, custodians, and lunchroom staff from school.

Suzy was known as a joker at school. She could always be counted on to make a sarcastic remark under her breath that would get other kids snickering in class.

Talk About It

- Do you have a blog? If so, what do you write about and who reads it?

- Do you read other people's blogs? Why do you read them and what do you like about them?

Once Suzy began to post about people from school, her blog got three times as many daily hits. People would approach her at school, laughing, about something she'd posted the day before. Pretty soon, people from every grade were reading it. She felt almost like a celebrity at her junior high.

Because people had liked her posts about teachers and other faculty at school so much, she figured they'd probably get a kick out of reading about other students. She chose only the easiest targets to write about. She made fun of the super short kid, Martin, and said he bought his pants in the little boy's section. She joked that the strongest girl on the basketball team would probably beat up the entire football team by the end of the year. People continued to read her blog and talk about how hilarious it was.

Suzy sometimes felt a little guilty about things she posted, but she pushed those feelings aside because everyone seemed to think the posts were so funny. She even told herself that maybe the people she wrote about could see the humor in it too.

Talk About It

- **Why do you think Suzy chose to make fun of other students on her blog? What do you think she thinks or feels when she posts something she knows could hurt someone else's feelings?**

- **Why do the other kids continue to read and laugh at Suzy's blog?**

One day, Suzy posted about an older girl, Kathleen, who always wore a different colored scarf on her head. The entry said, "Is she trying to start a new trend or something? Someone should tell her that flowered head scarves aren't coming back any time in the next century!"

Suzy was expecting a barrage of jokes to erupt after the post, but no one commented. After a few hours, she started to get a sinking feeling that she'd gone too far. Was this head scarf girl really cool or something? Finally, she received one post: "Suzy, we always knew you were nasty, but we didn't know you were an idiot! Kathleen has brain cancer!"

After a few hours, she started to get a sinking feeling that she'd gone too far.

Suzy couldn't believe the words staring at her from the computer screen: brain cancer. She had just made fun of a girl who was suffering from cancer. She felt worse than she'd ever felt before.

Talk About It

- Have you ever said or done something so mean that you felt terrible about yourself? Describe that feeling. Did you do anything to fix the situation?

- Have you ever encouraged someone else to make fun of an "easy target"? How did you feel?

Suzy felt horrible the more she thought about it. She didn't feel bad just about Kathleen—she felt bad about mean things she posted about other kids at school, teachers, and even celebrities. She realized she had to do something to make up for the fact that she'd been such a bully. She decided to make a public apology.

After deleting every mean thing she'd ever written about someone, Suzy posted an apology to Kathleen and the other victims of her cruel humor, and vowed to change her blog into things that were funny to everyone, not just making fun of people. She knew she could never take back what she'd done, but she could choose not to make the same mistake again.

Talk About It

- **Do you think Suzy did the right thing? What would you have done if you were in her position?**

- **How do you think Kathleen felt when she read the original entry? How do you think she felt after reading Suzy's apology?**

Some kids get easily carried away with bullying, especially when other kids egg them on. Bullying can be subtle—like teasing someone—but it is not always harmless. Although a bully might get attention and laughs from other kids when she is making a mean comment or playing a cruel joke, she will likely find that their interest doesn't last. She may find herself in a negative cycle of trying to do and say meaner and more outrageous things all the time just to get a laugh. Constantly focusing on the negative, she may start to feel pretty bad about herself and those around her. Plus, others may keep their distance for fear they will become her next target.

Suzy found that she could communicate mean ideas and jokes to lots of kids very quickly through her blog, and she took it way too far. She became untrustworthy. She may not have intended to hurt anyone, but she did. Fortunately, the experience shocked her enough that she chose to do the right thing by owning up to her mistake and changing the content of her blog.

Get Healthy

1. If you notice that another kid in your class is being targeted online, make a statement that you disagree with the bullying by posting something nice on his or her MySpace

page or Web site. It could be something simple, such as "I like the layout you used" or "It looks like you're having tons of fun in this picture." When other kids see that not everyone agrees with the teasing, they may stop it.

2. If someone posts something nasty about you online, avoid participating in a public debate. Instead, send a private message to the person who posted it explaining how it made you feel. Or better yet, talk to her in person.

3. If you are uncomfortable with a mean e-mail that has been forwarded to you about someone else, delete it instead of sending it to more people.

The Last Word from Ashley

Even though targeting people on the Web may be a common pastime among your class-mates, you still have plenty of opportunity to exercise your right to be nice online. Instead of participating in unfair bashing, use blogs and online communities as a way to show the world how much you care about your friends and other interests. Feeding the negativity will only lead to feeling crummy and making others feel worse. Choose to put the Web and other technology to good (and kind) use.

3
Clueless Parents

In this day and age, most people are networked and connected in every aspect of their lives through e-mail, cell phones, or online. Cell phones have become so sophisticated that we can take photos and videos, watch a favorite television program, or find ourselves on a map, all in the palm of our hand. As we become more used to advanced technology as a part of our everyday lives, we also become more dependent on it.

Sometimes it's hard to imagine life before cell phones or the Internet. How did people get by without being able to call someone when they arrived to meet them? How long did it take them to do their homework when they were writing everything by hand? You don't have to look too far to find the answers to these questions: just ask your parents. Most of your parents got through middle school, high school, and college before the Internet was widely used.

Of course, many parents have quickly jumped into the digitized, modern world of technology. Some are as clued into texting, browsing, and surfing as their sons and daughters. But just as your mind might be boggled at the concept of life before cell phones, there are still some parents who don't get why their kids should require a personal cell phone or a computer. They might believe that because they got by without it, their kids can too.

It can be hard to be the only one in your group of friends without access to a cell phone or the Internet. Find out how Gabby learned to deal with her parents' views, and got them to understand her modern sensibilities a little better.

> **It can be hard to be the only one in your group of friends without access to a cell phone or the Internet.**

Gabby's Story

Gabby was the oldest in a family of four kids. Her parents were way into organic food, yoga, and natural medicine . . . and not into modern technology. They believed that dependence on the Internet and cell phones created distance and destroyed communication between people, so Gabby wasn't allowed to have either. This frustrated her to no end.

She could not understand how her parents thought that these things that were meant to enhance communication actually destroyed it. *She* was the one who felt out of the loop when talking with her friends at school because she hadn't downloaded a popular song or read someone's latest blog entry. Gabby's friends found it hilarious that she still had to call them from a landline at home instead of a cell phone. Some of their families didn't even *have* landlines anymore.

Talk About It

- **Do your parents have rules about using certain kinds of technology, such as the Internet or cell phones?**

- **How do you feel when your parents restrict you from doing or having something you want? What do you do about it?**

Gabby tried to catch up on e-mails and Web sites when she went to her friends' houses, but it didn't seem like enough. She even had to stay late at school to use the Internet in the library just to complete her homework assignments. When she complained to her parents about this, they just shrugged their shoulders and said that it "builds character" to have to work for

things instead of having everything at one's fingertips and taking it for granted.

Talk About It

- Do you agree or disagree with Gabby's parents' view that it builds character to work for things?

- Think of a time when you had to go out of your way to get something done. How did it make you feel once you had accomplished the task?

One Friday, Gabby was supposed to go out with her friends to a movie after her dentist appointment. The appointment ended up running late, and her

mom had to stop at the store on the way home. Gabby was getting nervous because she knew everyone would be making plans for rides around 5:00 p.m. By the time she got home, it was already 6:00 p.m. She ran inside and began frantically dialing her friends, but no one was picking up. Finally Keisha answered her cell phone and told her that they had already left for the movie because they couldn't get in touch with her.

After she hung up the phone, Gabby was fuming. If only she had a cell phone, she could have called and let them know where she was! She began screaming at her mother.

"I'm the only one without a phone! It's not fair! Just because you think cell phones are evil, doesn't mean I have to!" Her tone was taunting and angry.

If only she had a cell phone, she could have called and let them know where she was!

"If you would lower your voice and ask politely, Gabby, I would drive you to meet your friends," replied her mother, calmly. But that only made Gabby angrier.

"I don't want you to drive me anywhere! You're ruining my life!" Gabby screamed and ran upstairs to her room.

Talk About It

- **Have you ever missed an activity because you were busy with family stuff?**

- **Do you think it's fair for Gabby to say her mother is "ruining her life"? What else could she have said to get her point across?**

Once she calmed down, Gabby realized that perhaps she'd gone too far by yelling at her mom. But she was still frustrated and angry that she wasn't allowed to have the Internet or a cell phone. She knew she had to do something about it. She decided to start with the cell phone and made a list of all the positive reasons for having one.

Gabby approached her parents with the list. First, she apologized for her behavior earlier in the evening, noting that she had overreacted because she was frustrated. Then, she explained why having a cell phone would be a good idea: she could call her parents and check in when she was out with friends, she would work extra hours babysitting for her younger siblings to help pay the monthly bills, and she wouldn't tie up the landline every night chatting with her girlfriends.

After hearing Gabby's reasons, her parents told her that they appreciated how she had handled the situation maturely and had come up with reasonable arguments. They agreed to let her get a cell phone—with some restrictions. She was only allowed a limited plan because they didn't want her spending all her time on it, she couldn't take calls during dinner or family outings, and she had to help pay for it. Gabby was thrilled. Now that she'd convinced them to let her have a cell phone, she would start working on getting the Internet at home.

Talk About It

- Can you think of some other arguments for having your own cell phone? What are some arguments against it?

- Have you ever tried to persuade your parents to see things your way by presenting a list like Gabby did? Were you successful?

Gabby's parents were trying to do what they thought was best for their daughter, but it felt unfair and stifling to Gabby. Not having the same access to technology as her peers made her feel insecure and excluded. But Gabby proved that she was strong, independent, and thoughtful enough to have a cell phone. She contributed her own babysitting money to help pay for it and explained to her parents the benefits of cell phones. In order for daughters to resolve disputes with their parents, they need to understand what points can be agreed on and show that they can handle the privilege, like Gabby did.

Get Healthy

1. If your parents are against you having a cell phone, point out that it will be safer for you to have one in case of emergencies. See if you can get them to let you use one when you go out. Once they are comfortable with that, you may begin to gradually build your phone privileges.

2. Don't forget that technology is expensive. If you really want a cell phone, show your parents that you can manage money by saving up for it yourself or offering to contribute toward the monthly bill.

3. Share with your family a graphic design or let them listen to a song you made using computer software. This could help them see how you are using programs to learn and create something.

4. Borrow a game system from a friend and suggest playing a computerized game as a family. Choose something that is interactive and designed for all age groups. Your parents may begin to appreciate how modern technology could be incorporated into family time instead of taking away from it.

5. Remember to respect your parents' decisions about how much technology they allow in your family's household. And show you can handle their decisions with a mature attitude.

The Last Word from Ashley

Being the only one without the Internet and a cell phone could make a girl feel like she's speaking two different languages at home and with friends. But eventually, even parents who aren't so tech-savvy will probably understand some of the benefits of modern technology. Try to get your parents to see your point by taking responsibility and showing them you care what they think. Soon, you might find that those evenings reading by the fire as a family will include music playing from your new iPod!

4

The Online Shopper

odern technology really has changed people's lives. It allows us to do so many things, including running errands and paying bills, without having to move from where we are sitting. Shopping online has progressed to the point where a person can buy groceries to be delivered to her home with just a few clicks of a mouse. For most adolescents, shopping or bidding on online stores is a regular part of their Internet usage. Some kids even have access to their parents' credit cards.

Online shopping certainly has some advantages. Kids have more options when it comes to music and clothing. For example, a girl may be able to buy songs online from a band no one would ever know about if not for its MySpace profile. She could just as easily find a hand-knit scarf from a do-it-yourself Web site. She can easily compare prices to get the best deal. Even if she lives in a small town without many stores, she can still order clothes from catalogs online.

But e-shopping also has its downsides. Not every site is secure and credit card fraud can be a problem. Some online purchases become lost or stolen in the mail. Some girls find themselves developing shopping habits they can't support with a teenage allowance. They may begin to lie to their parents or feel out of control about shopping. Read on to learn one e-shopaholic's story.

Madison's Story

Madison was a fashionista just like her mom. The two of them went shopping almost once a week and always bought at least a few new things. Since her parents had quite a bit of money and always paid for everything, Madison never thought about the cost of new clothes, shoes, and bags. In fact, she rarely glanced at the price tag.

Since her parents had quite a bit of money and always paid for everything, Madison never thought about the cost of new clothes, shoes, and bags.

All of Madison's friends were jealous of her walk-in closet. It had an entire wall devoted to her shoes and a dresser filled only with designer jeans. At school, she was known as the girl with the best wardrobe. Sometimes, she noticed that her friends seemed slightly annoyed when she showed them something new she'd just purchased, but they always loved it when she gave away some of her clothes.

Talk About It

- **Have you ever been jealous that a friend got more new clothes than you did?**

- **Do you and your friends ever give each other your old clothes? What do you like or dislike about exchanging clothes with friends?**

As Madison's interest in fashion grew, she began to shop more and more online, in addition to the shopping trips with her mom. She used a credit card her parents kept in the kitchen for emergencies to pay for her purchases. Since Madison's parents were big spenders themselves, they didn't notice the extra charges right away.

Madison got even more attention at school for her clothes. She was wearing brand-new outfits almost every day. She found unusual things online that she

couldn't find shopping at regular stores with her mom. The more people noticed her extravagant and expensive clothes, the more Madison felt she had to impress them.

Talk About It

- Are your parents big spenders? How can you tell?

- How do you think your parents' spending habits affect the way you think about spending?

- Do you worry about impressing people with what you wear or how much money you spend on clothing? Why or why not?

Madison began to buy things online every few days. Some of the things would show up and wouldn't even fit her or would look totally different in person than they had looked on the Web site. It made her feel a slight twinge of guilt when she bought something she would never wear. She hid those items in the back of her closet so she wouldn't have to look at them.

Talk About It

- **Have you ever bought something that looked cute online, but when it showed up, it was ugly or didn't fit? What did you do about it?**

- **Have you ever hidden something you bought? If so, why?**

About a month after Madison began shopping so heavily online, her mother called her into the kitchen. She sounded angry.

"What happened to the kitchen credit card, Madison?" she asked.

Madison suddenly felt nervous. "I used it to buy some clothes I saw online," she admitted.

"Do you realize that I just received a bill for $5,000? That's for one month of shopping, Madison. Do you have any idea how much money that is?" Her mother was upset. Madison was surprised to hear how much she had spent. It sounded like a lot of money.

"I didn't know," she mumbled, guiltily.

"I hope you're happy with all of your new purchases, because you won't be getting anything else this year," her mom told her.

Madison couldn't believe it. Hearing how much she'd spent bothered her. She had been so concerned with buying things that she hadn't considered the consequences. Plus, she was worried that not having any new clothes would affect her reputation at school.

Talk About It

- **Do you think Madison's punishment is fair? Why or why not?**

- **Have you ever found yourself doing something without any thought of the consequences? What happened? How did you feel about it?**

At first, Madison was bummed out, but eventually she figured out a way she could keep her fashionista reputation without spending any money. She began mixing and matching all the things she had in her closet already. There was a lot to choose from.

Madison became creative with the clothes she owned. She learned to sew so she could alter the stuff that didn't fit or use the fabric to make new things. Eventually, she even started a blog that was all about

making her own look out of old or reworked clothes. It felt good to turn her interest in fashion into something creative—definitely much better than it had felt buying things just to buy them. Now, she looked at clothes online to get ideas for things to make herself.

It felt good to turn her interest in fashion into something creative—definitely much better than it had felt buying things just to buy them.

Ask Dr. Robyn

Because online shopping seems easy and somewhat detached in comparison to shopping at an actual store, girls sometimes exercise less restraint than they normally would. This is especially true if they have access to a credit card or have not been taught how to budget properly. For some adolescent girls, the sheer number of online stores and options becomes irresistible. They may feel like they need to have something simply because it is there. The ease and the speed at which they can make purchases doesn't provide much time to second-guess such impulse buys.

Early lack of control around online shopping can lead to major problems if not corrected, including serious credit card debt or a full-blown shopping addiction that may have to be treated professionally. It's important that parents teach their daughters to practice sound reasoning and self-control when it comes to shopping, and it's equally important that daughters see access to any financial means (such as credit cards) as a privilege that is not to be abused.

Get Healthy

1. Ask your parents to teach you how to budget, save, and spend wisely. These are skills you will need throughout your entire life!

2. Instead of buying a new top online, go through the clothes you already own to see if you can make any new outfits. Altering something to fit differently can be just as good as buying something brand new.

3. Save your money and turn your old junk into a piece of art or something new to wear. Make a mosaic tray or tabletop from broken plates or turn a Chinese takeout box into a purse.

4. Try the five-day rule: if you see something you really like and want to buy it, think about it for five days before you actually make your purchase. By that time, you will have given yourself enough time to think about whether it's something you truly need and want or just an impulse buy.

The Last Word from Ashley

Learn the smart rules to e-shopping so that you can take advantage of unique things that are available online without breaking your bank. Learn how to budget in advance for everything to help you control your spending. When your parents see that you can be trusted to make thoughtful decisions about money, they may decide to loosen the rules on where or how you shop. Don't forget that smart shopping usually equals better shopping.

5

The Gamer

Many kids get really into video games during elementary and middle school. There are tons of different games to choose from: sports, fighting, driving, even fantasy role-playing games where you can create characters and interact with other players virtually. Games such as Wii allow kids to physically act out the motion of hitting or rolling a ball, so it feels like they are actually playing tennis or bowling. Thanks to advanced technology and sophisticated programming, video games have never looked so realistic or been as intuitive to play as they are now.

With all the different options to choose from and games that seem to go on forever with hidden or sometimes unattainable levels, it's no surprise that so many kids are hooked on gaming. But just because games are fun doesn't mean they're always good for you. Have you ever noticed how kids sitting in a room playing a video game barely look at or talk to one another, and will hardly pay attention if a new person walks in? Even though gaming may seem like a social activity that one does with friends, it can become lonely after a while. As Ling discovered, the best way to game is in moderation.

Even though gaming may seem like a social activity that one does with friends, it can become lonely after a while.

Ling's Story

Ling was a gamer. She loved everything from old-school pinball machines and Donkey Kong to brand-new, advanced games she would order specially from other countries. Some of the games she liked were so complicated that her friends couldn't figure out how to play them.

When she first got into gaming, her parents tried to set rules for how many hours she was allowed to play per day. But after a while, they got tired of fighting with her about it all the time and decided that she could play as much as she wanted as long as it didn't affect her grades. So Ling made sure to get all her homework done during breaks and on the bus after school. That way, she could play video games every day that she didn't go to drama club.

Talk About It

- Do you have an interest that you really like and at which you are better than all your friends? What is it and how much time do you spend doing it?

- Have you ever played a game that blurred the line between fantasy and reality? What did you like or dislike about it?

Though Ling had been a gamer for at least three years, her hobby changed when she discovered a game named Portal. In Portal, Ling could personalize her playing character so that she was part action hero, part real girl. It was the coolest thing Ling had ever seen. The character in the game looked like Ling with the same color hair and eye shape, but more womanly with longer legs and a bigger chest. She could run like a snow leopard and sword fight like a samurai. But the thing Ling liked best about her character was that she could talk to the other players during strategy development. She could meet an allied character in a dark alley to discuss the next play, but communicate with her own voice through a headset. Just like drama club, she could take on different personalities.

Soon, Ling was playing Portal so late into the night that she barely slept and was groggy during the school day. She stopped working on her homework during breaks because she was too busy strategizing and daydreaming about the game. She even stopped caring about drama club, which she used to love, and skipped practice frequently in favor of playing Portal.

Talk About It

- Have you ever become so obsessed with something that nothing else seemed to matter? What made you obsessed and how did it make you feel?

- What would you think about Ling's interest in Portal if you were her parent or friend?

Ling's parents grew concerned about these sudden changes, and told her they wanted her to quit gaming. But this only made her more obsessed—she couldn't bear the thought of not playing Portal. It was the only thing she cared about.

Then, Ling's parents found out her grades were slipping. Soon after that, they received a concerned call from the drama coach. They **Then, Ling's parents found out her grades were slipping.** decided to intervene. There would be no more Portal, and no other games either.

"What am I supposed to do? This is my life!" Ling protested, in a fit of tears and rage.

"How about reading a book?" her father simply replied.

"A book! Are you kidding me? You're taking everything away from me!"

"Listen to yourself, Ling!" her mother broke in. "It's not us taking everything away from you—it's the games taking everything away from you! I haven't seen you show emotion like this in months. You don't even look like yourself—you have pale skin and dark circles under your eyes—and you look puffy from sitting all day long. You used to love going to drama club and care about school, and now it's like all you care about is this game."

Ling was surprised to hear her mother say these things. She hadn't thought about how the game was affecting her life or that she might actually be addicted to it. That scared her. But now that she considered it, she remembered how she used to love drama club and have more energy.

"Okay," Ling said finally. She wasn't happy about it, but she had a sneaking suspicion that her parents were right.

Ling saw a look of relief cross her mother's face. Maybe it wouldn't be such a bad thing to spend more time with friends and family instead of living in her Portal-dominated world.

Talk About It

- Do you think it was fair for Ling's parents to take away her gaming privileges? Why or why not?

- What do you think of Ling's response? Why do you think it scared her to think that she might be addicted to Portal?

- Do you think Ling will change her gaming habits? How might her habits change?

Video games are fun and sometimes they teach you important skills, such as hand-eye coordination, spatial reasoning, or problem solving. However, they can suck you in and can easily become addictive.

Like most addictive behaviors, gaming addiction can result in mood and appetite changes and tiredness. It can sometimes even lead to depression. The best thing that a person who has started to develop a problem with gaming can do is to make deliberate efforts to change her behavior. Replacing gaming with substitute activities, especially ones that involve interaction with other kids, is a good start. Parents and teachers can help by paying special attention to changes in kids' moods or activity level, and by setting and enforcing limits on gaming time.

Get Healthy

1. Seek out games that involve some kind of physical activity. Even though playing Wii tennis is never going to be the same as getting out on the court with a friend, at least you're moving around instead of sitting for hours at a time.

2. For every hour you spend playing video games, spend one hour playing outside and one hour learning or trying something new. This could be anything from reading a book to baking cookies to learning to sew.

3. Next time you're playing a video game marked "mature" or "violent," count the number of violent acts that happen over a period of time. You might be shocked at how much violence can be packed into just a few minutes of video game playing. Ask yourself and your friends how playing violent games might affect your feelings about violence and your reactions to violent behavior in real life.

The Last Word from Ashley

Video games are not all bad, but playing them all the time can be. Think about it: do you really want to be the kind of person who sits around all day staring at a television, not talking to anyone or thinking about anything else besides a video game? Put your game playing into perspective by following one basic rule: if you feel like you can't live without the game, then it's probably time to do just that. After all, life doesn't take place on a screen in front of you—it's all around you and offers a whole lot of things (besides video games) to experience.

6

The
Web
Prey

The Internet allows us the freedom to do so many cool things, such as shopping online, chatting with friends, and keeping an online profile. But there is a downside to freedom online. It is not uncommon for spammers or other online predators to steal credit card information that can be used to make fraudulent purchases. An enemy from school could take a photo off a Web site and alter it to show something that never happened. Even worse, kids are sometimes targeted and victimized by adults posing as other kids on chat groups or teen-oriented social networking sites.

With these potential pitfalls, it is no wonder that some parents become nervous about their kids visiting certain Web sites, posting pictures, or sharing information. Many parents have rules against joining online groups. Adolescent girls may also be a little freaked about the idea of some creep contacting them online. So how do you take advantage of all the awesome stuff online while still protecting yourself from the danger zones? Read on to learn how Callie answered that very question.

Callie's Story

Callie was in seventh grade, and like most of her friends, she went online almost every day to IM or shop for new sneakers. The one thing she wasn't allowed to do was have an online profile. Callie's parents didn't think it was safe for her to post photos and information about herself online because "some old creep" could see it.

Callie was endlessly annoyed by this rule. It seemed crazy that her parents would be so worried. So what if a stranger saw her picture? What was the worst that could happen? She argued with them about it constantly, but nothing she said seemed to change their minds.

It seemed crazy that her parents would be so worried. So what if a stranger saw her picture? What was the worst that could happen?

Talk About It

- Do your parents have any rules for what you can and can't do online? Why do they have those rules and how do you feel about them?

- Do you ever worry about "some old creep" seeing pictures or reading information about you online?

One day, when Callie was staying at her friend Ava's house, they decided to go online.

"Let's make a profile for you!" Ava suggested.

"I can't. My parents would be sooo mad if they found out! It's totally against their rules," Callie said, rolling her eyes.

"Oh come on! We could put it under a fake name. No one will ever know," Ava suggested.

Though Callie felt a little guilty about disobeying her parents, she decided that making the profile would be harmless as long as her parents never found out. Finally, she agreed to it.

Talk About It

- Have you ever disobeyed a major house rule? How did it make you feel? Did you ever get caught?

- Do you think making the profile is totally harmless as long as Callie's parents never find out? Why or why not?

Ava and Callie created a profile under the pseudonym Calico. They filled in information about her favorite music group and movie, and they added tons of people from school as friends. Almost as soon as they created her profile, people started accepting her friend requests, and others added her as a friend. This is great, Callie thought, suddenly feeling more popular. What could be so bad about this?

Callie couldn't tell by everyone's pictures who they were, so she accepted everyone who added her as a friend. She assumed they knew her. One random person she accepted, Kayla, started IM-ing her immediately.

"Hey girl! How r u?" Kayla wrote.

"Gr8! U?" Callie replied. She was IM-ing with four other people at the same time and not paying much attention.

"Prty cool. What r u doing 2nite?"

"Sleepover w/Ava."

"Ava Jones?"

"Yes," Callie wrote back.

"Does she live near you???" Kayla asked.

Callie looked at the screen. She had five IM boxes blinking at her, but the conversation she had going with Kayla was starting to get really weird. Why was Kayla asking so many questions? Callie started to feel nervous, especially when she realized that she didn't know anybody named Kayla.

"R her parents gonna be home?" Kayla asked again.

Who was this person? Why did she want to know where Ava lived and if her parents were going to be home that night?

"Who is this?" Callie wrote. Suddenly, Kayla logged off. Callie started to get really creeped out. Who was this person? Why did she want to know where Ava lived and if her parents were going to be home that night?

Right away, Callie told Ava what had happened. Ava thought it was weird, too, but she didn't seem as nervous about it as Callie was.

"It's probably just some boys from our class try-ing to mess with us," Ava suggested.

But when the two girls tried to go on Kayla's pro-file to see who she really was, it was blocked.

Talk About It

- Has anything creepy ever happened to you online? What happened and how did you handle it?

- Have you ever deleted an online profile? Why or why not?

The more Callie thought about what happened, the more it bothered her. After deleting Kayla from her friends, she decided to cancel her own profile.

At first, Ava thought Callie was being paranoid. But after Callie told Ava what her parents had said about old men faking their identity in order to meet young girls online, Ava started to get creeped out too. When Callie reminded her that "Kayla" knew her last name, Ava decided to delete her profile as well.

Soon after Ava and Callie deleted their profiles, they heard at school that the site they were on had put out a warning to young girls to be careful about protecting their identities. Apparently, the site was not secure and had become a hot spot for online predators. Callie decided that until she knew she could be safe from online predators, she would stick to private e-mailing.

Talk About It

- What do you think about the way Callie reacted to the weird activity? What do you think of Ava's reaction?

- Would you have handled it the same or differently?

- What is the worst that can happen online and how can you protect yourself from it?

All girls, no matter how Web savvy they are, need to be concerned about protecting themselves from online predators. It takes most online predators only a matter of minutes to locate all the vital information to reveal a girl's identity once he has access to her personal profile. Plus, most of the tricks girls use to protect their identity aren't foolproof—pseudonyms are out the window as soon as someone leaves a public comment calling a girl by her real name.

The best way to protect yourself from Web thieves or stalkers might be to avoid shopping, chatting, or making a profile online. But our culture is dependent on the Internet, and most adolescent girls will become vulnerable to its potential risks at some point or another. Parents might find they can protect their daughters better by keeping an open dialogue on Web activities, knowing who their daughter's online friends are, and setting ground rules for credit card usage. Girls can help keep one another safer by telling as many people as possible when they notice something shady happening online.

Get Healthy

1. Visit an Internet safety awareness group to educate yourself. Learn tips on how to protect yourself online and how to identify

a potential predator. Share your new knowledge with your classmates.

2. Sit down with your parents and go through your Facebook or MySpace account. Tell them who each of your online friends is and explain how you know them. This will make your parents less likely to snoop on your online account, and it will help protect you against anything unsafe that you may be overlooking.

3. Always avoid becoming friends or chatting with anyone online who you aren't sure you know and trust in real life. Be especially cautious if someone claims to be a friend of a friend.

4. Change your e-mail and other passwords on a regular basis to make it harder for people to log into your account.

The Last Word from Ashley

As annoying as it is to be forbidden from having a profile, recognize that your parents truly are looking out for your best interests. The more you show them how you are protecting yourself, the more likely they will be to allow you more privileges online. This can include everything from reading about telltale signs of online predators to visiting only protected sites. Remember, if you're going to be a true cyber chick, you've got to get some cyber smarts.

7

The Texter

What's the first thing you do when something funny happens? What about when you need to tell your parents that you'll be home late? What do you do if you have a question about a homework assignment? Chances are pretty good that you text someone. Text messaging has become one of the main ways people, especially kids, communicate. It's quick, easy, and accessible almost all the time. Texting is so fast and convenient that sometimes it seems easier than having a conversation in person. Texting allows a person to state a thought, get an answer to a question, or share a piece of information in a matter of seconds, without going through the formalities that sometimes seem necessary when using other forms of communication.

This instant gratification has made us dependent on texting. The downside of texting dependency is that it sometimes causes people to miss out on things. For example, even though you may find out immediately whether your friend can pick you up after practice via text message, she probably won't bother typing out the entire story about a funny thing that happened to her that day.

A girl can become so preoccupied with texting that she may not even pay attention to things that are going on immediately around her, such as a discussion at the dinner table or a glass wall she's about to walk into. As silly as it sounds, texting can actually be dangerous! Just take it from Vivienne.

The downside of texting dependency is that it sometimes causes people to miss out on things.

Vivienne's Story

Vivienne was an avid texter. She texted her friends about whether the boy she liked had asked about her, she texted her after-school schedule so her mom would know when to pick her up, and she texted her older sister, who was studying abroad in Europe. Vivienne was so into texting that she often found herself doing it during movies or while she was hanging out with friends.

Talk About It

- Do you text more than calling, e-mailing, or speaking in person? If so, what do you like about texting?

- Have you ever texted one friend while you were hanging out with another friend? How did the friend you were hanging out with react?

Recently, Vivienne had gotten into a habit of texting during class, even though she knew her phone could be taken away if she were caught. Usually, she did it when she was bored, but she sometimes felt like she had to reply right away if she got a text from one of her friends—it seemed rude not to.

Talk About It

- Why do you think Vivienne texts during class, even though she knows her phone could be taken away? Is it worth the risk? Why or why not?

- Have you ever felt like you had to reply to a text immediately? Are phone calls or e-mails any different? Why or why not?

One afternoon during a quiz in Mr. Grover's history class, Vivienne started getting texts from her friend, Ellen, from across the room.

"C looks HOT 2day," Ellen wrote.

Nervously, Vivienne glanced around the room before replying. She didn't like using her phone when everyone was quietly working. She worried that Mr. Grover might notice.

"Ttyl . . . got to finish this. So hard," Vivienne wrote, hoping that would stop Ellen from texting, at least until they'd handed in their quizzes.

But Ellen wrote back immediately. "I didn't study! Wht is the answr to #4?"

Now Vivienne was really conflicted. She didn't want to seem lame, and it seemed easy to give Ellen the answer. But even though she knew she might be able to get away with it, she didn't want to cheat. She decided not to respond.

About 30 seconds later, Vivienne got another text, "Do u know #4?"

About 30 seconds later, Vivienne got another text, "Do u know #4?"

Before she had a chance to think about responding, Mr. Grover grabbed Ellen's cell phone out of her hands.

"You know you're not supposed to use cell phones during class, Ellen." Mr. Grover sounded really angry. "What could be so important that you had to text about it right now?"

"Nothing," Ellen stammered, her head down. Vivienne's heart was beating fast. What if he looked at the text messages Ellen had sent to her?

"Sent to Vivienne," Mr. Grover read aloud from the phone. "Could that be Ms. Vivienne Parker, sitting across the room from you? 'Do u know #4?' Could that be the answer to question #4 on the quiz we are taking right now?"

Vivienne could see that tears had begun to streak down Ellen's face. Meanwhile, Mr. Grover was absolutely fuming.

"Another text to Vivienne, 'I didn't study! Wht is the answr to #4?' I take it that Ms. Parker did not respond to your cheating text messages, then?"

Ellen didn't respond.

"I'm confiscating this cell phone. You can take a trip down to the principal's office, Ellen."

Vivienne couldn't believe this was happening, and that she had managed not to get into trouble or have her phone taken away. When class was over, she tried to duck out as quickly as possible, but Mr. Grover caught her on the way out.

"Ms. Parker, I applaud you for not cheating. However, you will not learn anything in my class or anyone else's if you continue to spend all your time text messaging. Turn off your cell phone when you're here."

Vivienne agreed to do as Mr. Grover asked. Maybe text messaging had been distracting her from Mr. Grover's lectures, but this event had taught her something pretty important. She realized that she didn't always use her best judgment when she was busy texting. Even though she'd gotten away unscathed this time, next time she could get into even more trouble. From now on, texting at school was off-limits.

Talk About It

- Do you think it is fair that Ellen's phone was taken away but not Vivienne's?

- What do you think about the way Mr. Grover handled the situation?

- Have you ever had something personal that you wrote, such as a note, be read aloud during class? If so, how did you feel when that happened?

Vivienne did the right thing by listening to her internal voice of reason and not replying to Ellen's texts. But it was a close call. Vivienne had become so wrapped up in her texting habit that she started to lose perspective on when it was appropriate and inappropriate to text. She even started to feel obligated to reply to her friends right away.

One of the problems with our text-obsessed culture is that people send messages back and forth so rapidly that they sometimes don't think carefully about what they are writing. And even worse, some people don't pay attention to what they are doing when they are texting—like driving down the road. How terrible would it be to hurt yourself because you tripped while texting, or to get into a car accident because you couldn't look up from your cell phone? The best way to keep texting in check is to establish for yourself when it's okay and not okay to text.

Get Healthy

1. Make a point to put your phone down when you walk, bike, or drive. Even though texting seems harmless, it can trip you up or cause

an accident. Driving while texting or using a cell phone is illegal in some states.

2. Lock your phone when you're not using it. It will make it slightly less convenient to grab it to send a text, plus you won't accidentally dial people.

3. Handwrite a note to a friend on a homemade card. They'll be touched that you took the effort to actually make something instead of simply reaching for the phone.

The Last Word from Ashley

You don't want to spend so much time texting that you miss the best part of a movie or fall down the stairs, right? Remember, you have to actually participate in life instead of just repeating what is happening over text message. So ditch the phone every once in a while and you may find you actually have stories worth texting about.

8

Taboo Web

aving technology smarts covers social networking sites to e-shopping to gaming to texting. But what about the thing that makes the Internet so fascinating, and also sometimes scary? The Internet is where people can find taboo content, especially sexual and violent content. In the past, people went to out-of-the-way specialty stores to get taboo material, or they risked the chance of being seen buying or viewing something obscene. Now, everything is readily available within the privacy of the home. This has caused quite different reactions. More "mainstream" people are viewing or posting taboo material online. And more people are reacting to this type of content with fear and concern about what their children might be exposed to. Many have gone so far as to block certain Web sites in an effort to shelter kids from pornography and violent content.

Despite censorship efforts, kids can still find taboo content online fairly easily. How does taboo content affect the average adolescent girl? Chances are, she falls somewhere in the middle of actually participating on taboo Web sites and trying to shut them down. Like most kids, she's probably both curious and freaked out about what she might find on such a site. Perhaps she feels unsure about what kind of image she should be presenting of herself online when women on the Internet are portrayed as so over-the-top sexual. Learn how Jeri discovered what felt comfortable and uncomfortable for her after viewing taboo material online.

> **Perhaps she feels unsure about what kind of image she should be presenting of herself online when women on the Internet are portrayed as so over-the-top sexual.**

Jeri's Story

Jeri was a typical girl from the West Coast. She was interested in friends, school, clothes, and boys, in that order. When she wasn't studying, she spent most of her time with one or two close girlfriends.

Jeri's parents had downloaded software on their home computer that blocked certain sites, so neither she nor her younger brother could access anything "bad." Jeri didn't know exactly what they meant by "bad," but for some reason, she felt uncomfortable asking her parents for an explanation.

Talk About It

- **Does your family block anything on the home computer?**
- **What do you think Jeri's parents mean by "bad?"**
- **Why do you think Jeri feels uncomfortable asking her parents for an explanation of what "bad" means?**

One day, Jeri was hanging out at her friend Leigh's house. They decided to go online. They started out on their favorite clothing site, choosing outfits for their Christmas wish lists. After that, they browsed a celebrity gossip site for a while, but soon they began to grow bored.

"There's nothing new on here," Leigh complained.

"Do you want to put in a DVD or something instead?" Jeri suggested.

"Or . . . we could go to the dirty sites," Leigh grinned mischievously.

"Like what?" Jeri asked. She knew these were the "bad" sites her parents had blocked at home. She felt a mix of excitement and nervousness.

Talk About It

- Why does Jeri feel a mix of excitement and nervousness?

- Have you ever visited a "dirty" site? Was it easy or difficult to get to these types of sites?

- What did you see, and how did it make you feel?

"You'll see," promised Leigh. Sure enough, Leigh already knew about a bunch of sites she could get on without proving to be 18 years of age.

At first, Jeri wasn't too surprised at what she saw—mostly just a bunch of naked girls—but as Leigh clicked further, there were videos and other images of the girls doing things Jeri had never seen before. Some of them didn't look much older than herself.

Jeri had a queasy feeling in her stomach looking at the images, and yet she couldn't seem to look away. She and Leigh cracked jokes and made fun of the people in the photos, which made the whole thing seem less awkward.

Talk About It

- **Can you think of a time when something made you feel sick but you couldn't seem to look away?**

- **Have you ever used jokes to make a situation feel less awkward? How or why did joking help?**

Pretty soon, Jeri started acting out exaggerated versions of the girls' positions. She and Leigh cracked up in hysterics.

Leigh grabbed her digital camera and aimed it at Jeri. "Do it again!" she giggled.

Jeri posed for the camera, laughing from the floor. The sillier she acted, the more they laughed.

"Okay, now do a real one. Make a real sexy face," Leigh instructed. But this made Jeri feel weird. Joking around was one thing, but acting like she meant it was another.

"I don't know . . . I feel like an idiot," she protested.

"Oh, c'mon," Leigh prompted.

With hesitation, Jeri tried her best to make her face look like the girls she'd seen online. She tried pushing her chest out and pursing her lips as Leigh egged her on, but eventually she started to feel really self-conscious and quit.

With hesitation, Jeri tried her best to make her face look like the girls she'd seen online.

Talk About It

- **Have you ever tried to imitate a sexy pose? If so, did it make you feel uncomfortable at all?**

- **Why do you think Jeri keeps playing along, even though she feels self-conscious?**

"Okay, I'm done with that game," Jeri announced. She hoped that Leigh would forget about the photos and want to do something else.

"Let's look at them!" Leigh suggested as she immediately uploaded the photos onto the computer. They laughed as they looked through the first ones. But when they got to the one where Jeri had made a sexy face, the laughter subsided.

Leigh said, "You look really pretty here. You should make this your profile picture."

Jeri looked at the photo in surprise. She'd never seen herself quite that way before. A part of her was proud that she resembled the girls online, but another part felt shy. She wasn't sure she wanted anyone seeing that photo, not even Leigh.

"No, I don't think that's a good idea. I look ridiculous. I think we should delete it," Jeri told Leigh.

Talk About It

- **Have you ever been surprised to see yourself in a new way? What about the picture makes Jeri feel proud and shy at the same time?**

- **Have you ever posted a sexy photo of yourself online? If so, why did you post it?**

- **How did people respond to the photo? Did you like or dislike their response, and why?**

Leigh seemed disappointed to delete the photo, but Jeri insisted. She was glad to have made that decision later when she saw that Leigh had posted a photo

of herself posing sexy on her profile. Jeri realized that she didn't want to try so hard or to act like someone she wasn't to get attention. She'd rather that people liked her for herself.

Talk About It

- Do you think posing sexy for an online profile is trying too hard or acting like someone you're not? Why or why not?

- Why do you think Leigh was pushing so hard for Jeri to post the photo?

Ask Dr. Robyn

Taboo images are becoming more familiar to our everyday experience, but that doesn't lessen their impact on adolescent girls growing up and defining themselves. Imitation is one way that adolescent girls try on different roles and images. Of course, many girls imitate images of women they see in the media, which tend to be highly sexualized and extremely thin. Many girls feel insecure to find they don't measure up to unrealistic images of female beauty and body types. Some reject such images, or even reject the idea that they have their own unique beauty and sexuality, until they are much older. Others take on the persona of a highly sexualized woman, which can lead to sexual attention they may not be ready for.

The Web offers the freedom to play with, reject, or embrace these images, which can be both good and bad. Talking regularly with trusted adults and other girls can help an adolescent girl sort through how she feels about herself in relation to images online. This will help her learn to feel comfortable in her own skin like Jeri, without playing to the camera.

Get Healthy

1. Look for images of girls doing things you like to do, such as painting, skiing, or laughing. Compare these images to those of women

in skimpy clothing posing for the camera. Ask yourself which images you relate to more, and which represent the kind of girl you want to be.

2. Next time you watch television, count the number of violent and sexual images you see in a half-hour time period. Ask your friends to do the same. Pay attention to when these images are shown, and write down your observations.

3. Remember that your parents set rules for you because they care about your well-being. If you have a question about a rule they have made, be open and discuss it with them honestly.

The Last Word from Ashley

As cool as it is to have access to so many different media sources at all times, sometimes it can also feel a little overwhelming. This is especially true when it seems like there are images of perfect but totally unrealistic-looking women everywhere we look. Even though we can't always escape these types of images, we can make choices that will affect how many of them rub off on us. So the next time you feel sick of following the crowd, don't post the typical sexy photo. Do something totally original and unexpected instead and be prepared for an awesome reaction.

9

Danger Sites

The Internet has created a space for all kinds of small communities, or subcultures, to connect and discuss issues that are important to them. Web-based communities often do a lot of positive things. For example, activists interested in helping endangered animals can share information and raise money through the Web sites of nonprofit organizations. Politicians, businesspeople, entertainers, artists, and many others can all find online groups to connect with. They can share their ideas over the Web with people who they may never get the chance to meet in real life.

Because the Internet can bring together people from all over the world, there are also plenty of communities interacting online that could be dangerous. There are online communities for people who purposely cut, burn, or mutilate themselves; suicide Web sites; and sites that encourage drug abuse. One Internet community that has become popular among adolescent girls is known as "pro-ana" or "pro-anorexia." There are several hundred pro-anorexia Web sites, blogs, and groups, and most of them aim to encourage participants to starve themselves or force themselves to throw up after meals. Girls on pro-anorexia sites share tips to avoid eating and give "thinspiration" to maintain an unhealthy weight and lifestyle.

Even though most people agree that pro-anorexia sites encourage self-destructive behavior, some of them provide a space for girls who are struggling with eating disorders to talk to others with similar problems. Sometimes, girls even encourage one another to seek help. Because girls often feel embarrassed or ashamed of having an eating disorder, they may turn to pro-anorexia sites in order to feel less alone. But, as Julia discovered, participating on these sites often takes girls further down the path of unhealthy behavior.

Because girls often feel embarrassed or ashamed of having an eating disorder, they may turn to pro-anorexia sites in order to feel less alone.

Julia's Story

Julia had struggled with her eating habits for some time. She first began dieting at age ten, and lost weight while other girls her age were growing and becoming heavier. She became so thin in sixth grade that her parents took her to see Debra, a counselor. Debra helped Julia get on a meal plan and regain the weight that she'd lost. Even though Julia felt better and had more energy when she ate normally, she still secretly wanted to lose weight again.

Julia began to look up dieting tips online, and found herself reading a blog that gave instructions on exactly what she could eat every day and not gain weight. As she read further, Julia realized that the blog was created by a girl just slightly older than she was. "Marta" posted photos of herself, in which she appeared incredibly thin. In most of the photos, you couldn't see Marta's face, just close-ups of her tiny waist with her ribs showing or her shoulder blades jutting out. Sometimes, Julia was shocked and even disturbed by these images. But there was another part of her that couldn't help wishing that she, too, were stick thin.

Talk About It

- Do you think Julia's history contributed to her interest in pro-ana sites? Why or why not?

- Have you ever been on a danger site that encouraged self-destructive behavior? What led you to visit it and how did it make you feel?

Every day, Marta posted everything she ate for the entire day—which was hardly anything—and wrote about how she felt. Some days when she ate a regular-sized meal, she wrote things like, "I feel so bloated and fat, I just want to throw it all up."

Julia noticed that lots of people were commenting on the blog. A few people wrote things like "You're sick and you need help," but most of the comments encouraged her thoughts and behaviors. One girl commented, "Bones are beautiful, you are beautiful."

Talk About It

- **Why do you think Marta posts her entire diet every day? Why do so many people comment about it?**

- **How do you think both kinds of comments affect Marta? How do you think these comments affect other people reading the blog?**

- **If you had a strong desire to be skinny, like Julia does, how would you feel about Marta's blog?**

Sometimes, it seemed to Julia that they were competing over more than just who was the skinniest—they were competing over who had the worst eating disorder.

Deep down, Julia knew the sites were not good for her, but she couldn't seem to stop herself from reading them. Julia started to read Marta's blog every day. Eventually, she clicked on links from the blog to other similar blogs and sites. It seemed as if a lot of the girls posted the same types of things, mostly lists of what they'd eaten and photos of themselves or ultra-skinny celebrities. Sometimes, it seemed to Julia that they were competing over more than just who was the skinniest—they were competing over who had the worst eating disorder.

Talk About It

- Why do you think Julia reads the sites even though she knows they aren't good for her? Have you ever done something like this?

- Why do you think the girls on the pro-ana sites might compete over who has the worst eating disorder?

After a while, the things that Julia read on the blogs began to creep into her mind when she wasn't reading them. She would think about how one of the pro-ana girls said that eating the sugar in bread would make you fat. Julia then threw her sandwich away. She began to do exercises in secret in her bedroom after she read about how one pro-ana girl did 500 push-ups and sit-ups every day. Julia's parents had also noticed that Julia was spending a lot more time online lately. When they questioned her about it, she just told them that she had been assigned a lot of homework in her history class, and she was spending the time doing research.

It made her feel sad that she lied to her parents, but she didn't want them to discover the truth and say something to Debra. Even though Julia continued to see Debra on a monthly basis, her weight began to slip.

Talk About It

- **Why do you think the pro-ana sites are affecting the way Julia thinks and acts?**

- **Have you ever found a Web site that affected the way you thought or acted? What happened?**

- **Do you think it was okay for Julia to lie to her parents about her time online? Why or why not?**

Debra caught on to Julia's weight loss pretty quickly and asked her about it. Julia denied that anything had changed, saying that she was just busy and hadn't had time to eat. Debra pushed further.

"Julia, is there anything in your life that has changed recently? Anything you're doing differently that could be affecting how you feel about your body?"

Julia felt ashamed of herself for going on the pro-ana sites. She was reluctant to tell Debra after all the progress she'd made following her sixth-grade skinny phase. But she also didn't want to go back on a meal

plan or end up in a treatment facility like some of the girls she had read about. She decided to tell the truth.

"Have you ever seen any Web sites about anorexia?" Julia looked down when she asked Debra the question.

"Ahhh. You've found the pro-anorexia sites," Debra said. Julia was surprised that Debra knew exactly what she was talking about. "You know, those sites might seem harmless. You might even feel like you can relate to the girls on them as if they were your friends, especially after what you've been through. The problem is that they can take you right back where you just came from. Reading about calories and diets all the time could make you obsess and become anxious about food."

Julia knew exactly what Debra was talking about. Ever since she started reading pro-ana sites, she was worrying about calories more. She knew that she had to stop going on the sites and blogs.

Debra gave her some links to sites for eating disorder recovery instead. Julia began to read them and found that there were girls' stories much like her own, except that instead of continuing to give into their eating disorders, these girls were finding ways to get and stay healthy. Instead of feeling guilty, Julia felt more at peace with herself.

Talk About It

- **What do you think about the choice Julia made to come clean with Debra?**

- **Do you agree with Debra's advice? Do you think there is a possibility that a pro-ana blog could push someone to diet dangerously or develop an eating disorder? Why or why not?**

There is no way to monitor all Web-based material, so there are plenty of communities online that encourage dangerous and self-destructive behavior. While simply reading a pro-anorexia, pro-drug, or pro-cutting site is probably not enough to make every girl try these behaviors, these online communities can be extremely seductive to girls who are already vulnerable to the behavior. That's because communities like these tend to make the behavior, or the illness, seem like a cool, secret club. Instead of seeing that her behavior is potentially dangerous, a girl might decide to give into it in order to be part of the Web community. Many girls may need to seek professional help to deal with the thoughts, urges, and behaviors that led them to these sites in the first place.

Get Healthy

1. Pay attention to your instincts while viewing online material. Feelings of nervousness, fear, or the need to keep secrets could be warning signs that something is wrong.

2. Eating disorders are extremely dangerous and often deadly. If you or someone you know is engaging in strange eating habits or has recently lost a lot of weight, talk to your school counselor immediately. Be cautious of complimenting your friends for losing

weight—you could be encouraging disordered eating.

3. Instead of frequenting sites that encourage unhealthy behavior, visit sites for recovery and developing healthy habits.

4. If you find yourself caught up on sites that encourage dangerous behaviors or pull you toward things you've struggled with, talk to a trusted friend or adult about it.

The Last Word from Ashley

We've all had times when we've wanted to be part of a club, particularly one that seems mysterious, secret, or even slightly rebellious. Most of us have experienced a time when we went through pain or difficulty and we needed someone to understand us. Danger sites, such as those created by the pro-ana community, can make you feel like you're part of a club where everyone understands your pain. The problem is that instead of helping you feel better and get through a hard time, they may keep you in a dark place. No Web site is going to be there for you like your family and friends. Be strong enough to be honest with the people who really care about you, and sign off from the negativity.

A Second Look

We live in a cyber culture. Cell phones, online communities, and interactive games allow us to communicate with our friends and families, as well as people we may never meet in real life. We have access to more information than we could ever possibly absorb. We can virtually visit different places and times, and share our experiences through just a few quick strokes on a keyboard. We can get to know a girl in China or Madagascar by reading her blog, or play a game of tennis without picking up a racket.

The world is open to us at all times through advanced technology, which means that we are also open to it every time we log on to a site or send a text. Even though it might feel safe and harmless to send messages or post online, most of the girls in this book learned that they had to make a few rules in order to get safe fun out of the Internet and cell phones. Madison discovered that using fashion on the Internet as inspiration to create new outfits was far better than obsessive e-shopping. Ling realized that all the hours she spent playing Portal were hours spent away from her friends, family, and the activities she loved. Suzy determined that cyber bullying could be just as harmful as any other bullying. Jeri decided to skip out on posting a too-sexy profile picture that didn't represent her true personality. And Gabby finally convinced her non-techie parents to let her

enter the modern age of cell phones by showing them that she was responsible enough to
have one.

Whether you use interactive devices and
tools to help with a homework assignment,
send photos to friends, or listen to your music library, always be safe and tech-savvy.
Remember, cyber girls never let modern technology get in their way—they work it!

XOXO,
Ashley

Pay It Forward

Remember, a healthful life is about balance. Now that you know how to walk that path, pay it forward to a friend or even to yourself! Remember the Get Healthy tips throughout this book, and then take these steps to get healthy and get going.

- Make sure to use different passwords for different online accounts.

- Keep information you post online vague. Avoid specific information such as last names, phone numbers, addresses, school names, or mascots.

- The next time you play a violent video game or watch someone else play one, pay attention to the players' moods afterward. See if you notice any changes that might be caused by the game.

- Make a list of telltale signs of online predators, such as asking a lot of personal questions for no apparent reason or making contact without any prior relationship. You might find these on online safety Web sites or you may come up with them on your own. Share your list with your friends.

- Set your online profiles to private, so only your friends can view your photos or information.

- Upload new anti-virus and anti-spyware software and update regularly to protect your operating system.

- Before posting any photos or information on your personal profile, ask yourself if you would feel uncomfortable if your parents, grandparents, teachers, and coaches saw it. If the answer is yes, then don't post it.

- Keep your phone on vibrate instead of ring. Know when to put your phone away and pay attention to the friends and family you're with.

- Before e-mailing or IM-ing personal info about yourself, ask yourself if you would share this info if you were talking to each other in person. This is a good rule to help you avoid disclosing too much online.

- Get comfortable with at least one Web safety site. Visit it regularly for tips and information to keep you in the loop about what to watch out for on the Internet.

- If you find yourself having to lie to cover your online habits, think about why you are lying. It might be that you are into something that isn't good for you. Come clean to your parents and tell them the truth. Being honest with them will show that you are responsible and trustworthy.

Additional Resources

Select Bibliography

Farmer, Lesley. *Teen Girls and Technology: What's the Problem, What's the Solution?* New York: Teachers College Press, 2008.

Goodstein, Anastasia. *Totally Wired: What Teens and Tweens Are Really Doing Online.* New York: St. Martin's Griffin, 2007.

Willard, Nancy E. *Cyberbullying and Cyberthreats: Responding to the Challenge of Online Social Aggression, Threats, and Distress.* Champaign, IL: Research Press, 2007.

Further Reading

Appleman, Dan. *Always Use Protection: A Teen's Guide to Safe Computing.* Berkeley, CA: Apress, 2004.

Schwartau, Winn. *Internet & Computer Ethics for Kids (and Parents & Teachers Who Haven't Got a Clue).* Seminole, FL: Interpact Press, 2001.

Willard, Nancy E. *Cyber-Safe Kids, Cyber-Savvy Teens: Helping Young People Learn To Use the Internet Safely and Responsibly.* Hoboken, NJ: Jossey-Bass, 2007.

Web Sites

To learn more about using technology responsibly, visit ABDO Publishing Company online at **www.abdopublishing.com**. Web sites about using technology responsibly are featured on our Book Links page. These links are routinely monitored and updated to provide the most current information available.

For More Information

For more information on this subject, contact or visit the following organizations.

Pew Internet and American Life Project

1615 L Street, NW, Suite 700, Washington, DC 20036
202-419-4500
www.pewinternet.org
Pew Internet is dedicated to researching how the Internet affects children, families, schools, and communities.

Teenangels

1 Bridge Street, Irvington-on-Hudson, NY 10533
201-463-8663
www.teenangels.org
Teenangels offers tips and advice about online safety and trains young women to give presentations to their peers about how to stay safe on the Internet.

Glossary

activist

A person who vigorously supports a cause, usually for social justice.

allied

Joined by agreement or common cause.

censorship

The banning or suppressing of something.

fraud

Deceit or trickery.

identity

The sense of self, providing sameness in personality over time.

intervene

To come between two or more things.

intuitive

A quality that refers to saying or doing something quickly and automatically without having to put much thought into it.

nonprofit organization

An organization that is legally responsible for improving resources or raising funds for a particular cause, rather than profiting its owners.

personalize

To make something one's own.

pornography

Videos, photographs, or text that feature graphic sex.

predator

A person who victimizes for his or her own gain.

progress

To advance toward a higher or better stage.

pseudonym

A fictitious name used to conceal a person's identity.

spammer

A person who sends unwanted or inappropriate electronic mail to multiple recipients, often advertisements.

subculture

A group within a society that has a shared set of customs, attitudes, and values, often with their own slang language.

taboo

Something that is looked on as improper or unacceptable.

unattainable

Out of one's grasp or impossible to achieve.

Index

About the Author

Ashley Harris lives and works in Chicago, Illinois, where she completed an MA from the University of Chicago. Her research focused on how Web culture has impacted adolescent girls' body image and sense of identity. Her work has appeared in *VenusZine* and *Time Out Chicago*. She enjoys live music, bike riding, and spending time with the many friends whose experiences helped her write this book.

Photo Credits